GW01182743

Published by Bradwell Books
9 Orgreave Close Sheffield S13 9NP
Email: books@bradwellbooks.co.uk

British Library Cataloguing in Publication Data:
a catalogue record for this book is available from
the British Library.

1st Edition

ISBN: 9781909914193

Print: Gutenberg Press, Malta

Design and artwork by: Andrew Caffrey

Photograph Credits:
Shutterstock and Kathryn Buchanan.

Bibliography
http://celticfc.net
www.chauncymaples.org
www.educationscotland.gov.uk
www.executedtoday.com
www.glasgowguide.co.uk
www.glasgowlife.org.uk
www.glasgowmuseums.com
www.nls.uk
www.rangers.co.uk
www.shinty.com
www.supernaturalscotland.co.uk
www.tripadvisor.co.uk
www.visitscotland.com

ARCHIBALD, M., Glasgow: The Real Mean City,
Black & White Publishing, Edinburgh, 2013
BARR, WILLIAM W., Ghosts of Glasgow, Richard Drew
Publishing Ltd, 1982
BARR, WILLIAM W., Glaswegiana, Richard Drew
Publishing Ltd, 1981
HOLLAND, RICHARD, Scottish Ghost Stories,
Bradwell Books, 2013
ROBINSON, RICHARD, History of Queen's Park Football
Club 1867–1917, published 1920

Acknowledgements:
I would like to thank everyone who contributed to this
book with their jokes, recipes and stories, especially
Tricia Lennan and Alasdair Sinclair. I would also like
to thank the staff at Provand's Lordship, the St Mungo
Museum of Religious Life and Art, the Willow Tea
Rooms in both Buchanan Street and Sauchiehall Street
and the staff and students at the Glasgow School of Art.

A special thank you to the very knowledgeable staff at
GoMA (the Gallery of Modern Art) and The Lighthouse.

Pictures © C Sanderson unless otherwise stated.

Bradwell's
ECLECTICA

GLASGOW

Kathryn Buchanan

BRADWELL
BOOKS

Contents

INTRODUCTION

Glasgow was once the 'Second City of the Empire', when 30 per cent of all the ships in the world were Clyde-built. Today it is a city of music, football and style, the UK's second favourite shopping city.

HUMOUR

Laugh out loud with these jokes and funny stories. Glasgow is famous for its sense of humor and the birthplace of many comedians including Billy Connolly and Kevin Bridges.

MURDERS

The doctor who poisoned his wife, the woman who murdered a paperboy and the murderer who took time to feed the victim's cat are just some of the terrible happenings in Glasgow.

LOCAL DIALECT

The patter is what you will hear in Glasgow, so to get up to speed you have to realise that messages are groceries and not emails, and the Subway is not a sandwich but the underground railway system.

RECIPES

Try our recipes for scotch pancakes, mince and tatties, clapshot and cranachan. Other Glasgow favourites are mince rounds, scotch pies, bridies and steak pies. A good place to buy these is the Countryside Family Butchers in the High Street.

LOCAL NAMES AND CLANS

Find out when surnames were first used in Scotland, the difference a capital letter makes after Mac, how Wilson's of Bannockburn marketed their tartan cloth and the origins of Crossmyloof.

WALKS

Two walks - Aroon the Toon: Find interesting buildings down narrow lanes and famous Glasgow landmarks and then **'The Merchant City'** which includes the Necropolis and Glasgow's oldest house.

LOCAL CUSTOMS

Seeing in the bells, first footin' and singing Auld Lang Syne are traditional ways of welcoming in the New Year, along with a wee dram and a bit of Madeira cake.

LOCAL HISTORY

Glasgow was ravaged by plaque and five years later, in 1652, suffered devastation again when a Great Fire spread through the city, destroying a third of the houses — fourteen years before the Great Fire of London.

GHOST STORIES

There are many spooky tales about Glasgow, including a lady who is said to sing in the Subway and a memorial in the Necropolis of a veiled lady who turns her head to keep watch over the grave.

LOCAL SPORTS

Although Glaswegians are mad about football, other traditional sports such as shinty and curling are very popular. The granite for curling stones comes from Ailsa Craig, an island in the Firth of Clyde.

FAMOUS LOCALS

There are many famous people associated with Glasgow and selecting just a few has been quite difficult. It's the people who make Glasgow, so perhaps we all deserve a mention — so here's to all Glaswegians, wherever you might be!

INTRODUCTION

George Square

Times have changed and so has the city. The old shipyards and the industry on the Clyde have all but disappeared and instead there are stylish walkways and architectural wonders such as the **ARMADILLO** and the **RIVERSIDE MUSEUM**. Avant-garde architecture is a traditional feature in Glasgow and there are not many cities with a Venetian-style carpet factory, such as the old **TEMPLETON'S BUILDING** and a Victorian/Art Nouveau style **HATRACK**, while **MACKINTOSH'S SCHOOL OF ART** still has a modern and exciting feel, despite being over one hundred years old.

Wellington dressed by Glasgow

statue has been a deterrent and Wellington, with his cone, is now ranked fifty-seventh in Tripadvisor's Glasgow attractions!

There are a few words and expressions to give you a head start with the patter. If told to **'HAUD YIR WHEESHT'** it would be good to stop talking as there is no

The Hatrack, St Vincent Street

Glaswegians like a bit of a blether, are hospitable and have a dry sense of humour, which can be seen in how they dress up the statue of **ROBERT BURNS** in George Square for his birthday celebrations on 25th January. The statue of Wellington, on his horse outside the **GALLERY OF MODERN ART**, mostly has a traffic cone on his head and sometimes other additions. Officials remove the cones with a high-powered water jet but neither this nor the fact that criminal charges may follow if caught climbing the

The Riverside Museum SHUTTERSTOCK/TARGN PLEIADES

way you will want a **'Glesga kiss!'** **'Haud the bus'** has nothing to do with transport but just means wait a minute. However, if you are on a bus, **'Com'on get aff'** means that you have arrived at your destination and it is time to get off the bus. Women should not be offended if they are called **'Hen'** as it is a term of endearment, and it is not rude to ask you if you would like a **'Pokey Hat'** as this is an ice cream cone. **'Ginger'** is any fizzy drink and Irn-Bru really does have iron in it – and 700 cans are bought in Scotland every minute.

The city's slogan can be seen even on taxis and it says, quite rightly, that it's the people who make Glasgow, so however much Glasgow changes it is still a friendly, welcoming and stylish city.

Kathryn Buchanan

SUBWAY IS NOT A SANDWICH BUT THE **UNDERGROUND RAILWAY SYSTEM!**

A

Ah – I
Affrontit – embarrassed
Are ye right? – Are you ready?
Auld – old
Away a place – dead
Aye – yes, always

B

Baggies – minnows
Bahookie – backside, bottom
Baltic – very cold
Bashed – mashed
Beamer – red face, blushing

Beat it – go away
Belong to – come from
Blether – chat, gossip

C

Chuffed – very pleased
Clarty – muddy, dirty
Close – entrance to a tenement

D

Dinnae – don't
Dug – dog

E

Embra – Edinburgh

F

Fankled – muddled, tangled, knotted
Frae – from

G

Gawk – stare
Geeza – give me
Ginger – any fizzy drink
Girn – moan, whine
Glesga kiss – head-butt
Greet – cry, weep

H

Haud the bus – wait a minute
Haud yir wheest – be quiet, stop talking
Hen – dear, love
Hoose – house

J

Jeely piece – jam or jelly sandwich

K

Ken – know

L

Links – sausages, bangers
Lug – ear
Lum – chimney

M

Manky – dirty, filthy
Maw – mum, mother
Messages – food shopping

N

Nae – none, no
Naeborra – no bother, no problem
Naw – no
Neeps – orange-fleshed turnips

O

Oose – fluff
Oot – out
Orrabest – all the best, good luck

P

Patter – talk, chat
Paw – father, dad
Pictures – cinema
Pinkie – little finger
Plank – hide or the hiding place
Poke – small paper bag
Pokey hat – ice cream cone
Polis – police

R

Ramorra – tomorrow

S

Shoogly – loose and shaky
Simmit – vest
Single end – one-room tenement flat
Skelf – splinter
Sook – suck
Stairheid – the landing in a tenement
Steamie – wash-house
Stoat – bounce

Stooky – a plaster cast
Stooshie – hullabaloo, big row
Subway – Glasgow underground railway system

T

Tatties – potatoes
Telt – told
Toaty – very small
Toon – town, Glasgow City Centre

U

Ur – are
Urnae – aren't

W

Wae – with
Wasnae – was not
Watter – water
Wean – child
Wee – small, young
Wheesht – be quiet
Windae – window

THE SAIR FINGER

by WALTER WINGATE *(1865–1918)*

WALTER WINGATE was born in Dalry, attended Glasgow University and graduated in mathematics before he was twenty years old. He became a schoolmaster and poet, with many of his poems being published in The Glasgow Herald, The Evening News and the Glasgow Ballad Club anthologies.

Ye've hurt yer finger? Puir wee man!
Yer pinkie? Dearyme!
Noo, juist you haud it that wey till
I get my specs and see!

My, sae it is – and there's the skelf!
Noo, dinna greet nae mair.
See there, my needle's gotten it oot!
I'm sure that wisna sair?

An' noo, tae make it hale the morn,
Pit on a wee bit saw.
And tie a bonnie hankie roun' it,
There noo, rin awa'.

Whit! Yer finger's sair ana'?
Ye rogue, ye're only lettin' on!
Weel, weel, then – see noo, there ye are.
Aw' row'd up the same as John.

OCH! ITS NO MA TURN FUR THE STAIRS AGAIN!

Tiled entrance to close

If yi lived up a close in a tenement in Glesga yi hid tae take yir turn of doing the stairs. There wis a rota fur every landin' so it wid be your turn every three or four weeks, depending on how many hooses on yir landin'. Ye wid sweep and wash the stairs from your landin' doon tae the next landin', no' up. If there wis a shared lavvy yi wid have tae clean that as well. Some stairs had a half-landin' and here they'd be a stair windae. In some parts of Glesga these windaes wid always be broken and in others they would have a nice wee net curtain so that had to be taken doon an' washed every noo and again. In some tenements there wid be white edges to the stairs, one on each side, painted on. Mostly it wis the women who took a pride in keepin' the shared stairs clean and they wid no be happy if sumwan wis no pullin' thir weight. In the close where we lived there wis nae door like they hiv noo and anywan could come oot and in and go up the stairs or oot the back. Sometimes in the morning a tramp would be sleeping on wan of the landings and maybe an extra wash with a bucket of disinfectant wid be needed if it wis your week on the stairs.

There wis a songsheet published by James Kay in Glasgow between 1840 and 50 and it wis sold fur a penny. Here is an abridged version of The Battle on the Stair.

THE BATTLE ON THE STAIR

Says Mrs Doyle tae Mrs Grant,
You'd better clean the stairs!
Ye've missed yer turn fur mony a
week, The neighbours a' did theirs!
Says Mrs Grant tae Mrs Doyle,
Ah'll tell ye Mrs Doyle, You'd better
mind yir ain affairs An' clean the
stair yirsel'.

Says Mrs Grant tae Mrs Doyle,

Ah'm sure it's no ma turn,
You've got a cheek tae order me,
There's no a woman born
That keeps a cleaner hoose than me,
An' mark ye, Mrs Doyle,
Just wipe yir mouth before you speak,
And gang and clean yirsel'.

Says Mrs Doyle? Ye dirty slut,
Who was it stole the beef?
What do you say? cries Mrs Grant,
Do you mean that Ah'm a thief?
Pay me the sixpence I lent you,
To treat big I at M'Gine,
And where's the blankets Ah lent you
The last time you lay in?

Says Mrs Doyle to Mrs Grant,
You very well do know,
The sixpence that you lent to me
Ah paid you long ago,
An' yir dirty ragged blanket,

As all the neighbours says,
Walked off home the other night,
Drawn there by bugs and fleas.

The Irish blood of Mrs Doyle,
It then began to rise,
She made a rush upon her foe
To tear out both her eyes.
The Highland pluck it did get up,
An' now said Mrs Grant,
Look neighbours, she has struck me
first, Ah'll give her what she wants.

At length the polis took them both,
As Ah have heard them say,
While they were fined ten shillings
each, Upon the following day,
Or go ten days to Bridewell
For to settle their affairs,
Where they would learn to clean
their cells
As well as clean their stair.

HUMOUR

Jimmy decided he'd had enough of working on the Glasgow buses. He wanted try something new and see a bit of the world so he took the train from the Central Station to London Euston and fell in love with the big red London buses. 'Champion,' he said to himself. 'This'ill dae fur me!' So he went alang tae the bus station and asked fur a job on the London buses. They were short of staff so the inspector said, 'Come on into the office and answer a few questions.' So Jimmy did just that.

'The first question', said the inspector, 'is what would you do if you had a rowdy passenger on the bus?'

'I'd put them off at the next stop', replied Jimmy.

'Very good,' said the inspector, 'and what would you do if you couldn't get the fare?'

Jimmy was quick to answer: 'Ah'd take the first two weeks in August.'

....

'Weel, Malkie, I don't know aboot you but ma wife's been on aboot dieting again and Ah'm starvin'. Look wit Ah've got in my pieces again – its that cottage cheese!'

'Dae you no know the best diet, Stevie?'

'Whit's that, Malkie?'

'It's the called the Whisky Diet. Ah tried it and Ah lost three days!'

....

Tourist: 'Gee, we've had a lovely time seeing all of Glasgow from the City Sightseer Bus but there was one thing we just couldn't understand.'

Glaswegian: 'What was that, hen?'

Tourist: 'When we were in George Square, it was full of men holding an empty whisky tumbler in their hands.'

Glaswegian: 'Och, that's jist because the weather forecast on STV said there'd be a nip in the air.'

....

Jeanie was having trouble with her computer again so she asked the office computer guy for some help. Pete came over to her desk and clicked a few buttons and swirled the mouse about and solved the problem. As he was walking away, Jeanie asked him what was wrong and he replied, 'It was an ID ten T error.'

'An ID ten T error? What's that in case I need to fix it again?'

Pete grinned and said, 'Haven't you ever heard of an ID ten T error before?'

'No,' replied Jeanie.

'Here, I'll write it down for you,' says Pete and he writes 'ID10T'.

....

Whit is the difference between visiting somebody in **Glesga** and somebody in **Embra?**

In **Glesga** you'll be asked if you would like a wee cuppa tea and in **Embra** they'll say, 'I expect you'll have had your tea?'

....

'Com'on, there's the sirens, Aggie, we need tae get aff tae the air raid shelter.'

There they were, very nearly at the Subway when Aggie screams, 'Wait a minute Jimmy, Ah'll hiv tae go back hame.'

Jimmy says, 'Ye canae dae that, hen, we're nearly there.'

'Ah hiv tae, Jimmy, Ah've forgotten tae put ma teeth in.'

'Com'on, Aggie, its bombs they're dropping, no sandwiches!'

Maggie was on another diet and she often bought an iceberg lettuce when she was in the supermarket, but over the weeks she saw that they were getting smaller and smaller so she thought she would go and ask the manager the reason.

'Excuse, me,' she says. 'I would like to know why your iceberg lettuces are getting smaller and smaller.'

'Global warming,' replied the manager.

Davie went to the doctor and when the doctor asked him what was the matter, Davie told him that he felt like a pack of cards. 'Then I'll deal with you later,' replied the doctor.

After being unemployed for ages, Tommy got a job at a ten-pin bowling alley in Glasgow. He was delighted and gave his wife a ring from his mobile.

Listen, hen, I've just got a job at the bowling alley.

'Ten pin?' asks the wife.

'Naw,' says Tommy. 'Ah think it's permanent.'

Wee Flora brought home her report from school and her mammy told her she was doing very well in everything except history.

'Well, maw, that's because the teacher keeps asking me aboot things that happened before Ah was born!'

Dougie was building a garden shed and he ran out of nails so he went to the ironmongers to buy some more.

'How long do you want them?' asked the shop assistant.

'Oh, Ah need tae keep them,' replied Dougie.

....

Hamish was down on his luck so he thought he would try getting a few odd jobs by calling at the posh houses in Whitecraigs. After a few no ways, a guy in one of the big hooses though he would give him a break so he says, 'The porch needs painting so I'll give you £50 to paint it for me.'

'Yir a life-saver, mister, Ah'll get started right away!'

Times passes until...

'There ye go, Ah'm aw done with the painting.'

'Well, here's your £50.'

'Thanks very much. And by the way, it's a Ferrari, no a Porsche!'

....

Did you see the ad in the The Herald for a full set of Encyclopaedia Britannica?

Aye, Jimmy's sellin' them 'cos he's just got married.

Whit's that got to dae with it?

He's no needing them any mair as he says the wife knows everything!

RECIPES

TASTY GLASWEGIAN TREATS FOR ALL TO EAT!

Scottish Pancakes

See **page 24** for recipe

Mince and Tatties

MINCE ROUNDS 2.60

ONION SCOTCH PIES 1.08

MINCE AND TATTIES

There are many variations of this dish but basically it is beef mince cooked in a pan and served with boiled potatoes or tatties and neeps mashed together which is called clapshot. Here is the Buchanan family version, which has changed and evolved over the years to be a tastier dish.

INGREDIENTS:
1 tablespoon of olive oil
1 large onion chopped
2 carrots sliced and chopped
450g (1lb) low fat Aberdeen Angus beef mince
1 tin of baked beans – low sugar variety
1 or two beef stock cubes
Salt and pepper to taste
Boiling water
A couple of teaspoons of cornflour
450g (1lb) potatoes, peeled
170g (6 oz) neeps, peeled and diced

PREPARATION:
1. Heat the oil in a large frying pan and add the mince and the onion. Stir until browned.
2. Add the carrots and the crumbled beef stock cubes and seasoning.
3. Add enough boiling water to cover, stirring to mix.
4. Cover and cook for about 45 minutes.
5. Then add the tin of baked beans and a little cornflour to thicken the gravy if necessary. Cook for another 3 or 4 minutes.
6. In the meantime steam the potatoes and the neeps for about 25 minutes until cooked.
7. Remove from the steamer to a warm bowl and mash them together, adding a little butter and milk, but don't make them too wet. Season to taste. Now you have a Buchanan version of clapshot!
Serve the mince with the clapshot.

Cranachan

SHUTTERSTOCK/ZI3000

CRANACHAN

This is a traditional Scottish dessert made with Scottish raspberries. It can be served for breakfast by omitting the whisky and using yogurt instead of cream. For a healthier dessert use crème fraîche instead of cream. It is usually served in a tall glass, or you can place all the ingredients on the table so that everyone can choose their favourite combination and you can then offer crème fraîche as well as cream. If you are doing this do not combine the oatmeal, raspberries and cream but serve them in separate dishes.

INGREDIENTS:
500g (1lb) Raspberries
85g (3oz) pinhead oatmeal
100ml (6 tablespoons) whisky
3 tablespoons of heather honey
600ml (1pt) double or whipping cream

PREPARATION:

1. Toast the oatmeal in a pan over a high heat and remove the dust.

2. Soak the toasted oatmeal in the two tablespoons of whisky overnight.

3. Keeping five raspberries aside for each glass, blend the rest and combine with the oatmeal, whisky, honey and cream.

4. Place three raspberries at the bottom of the glasses and add the mixture.

5. Chill before serving and then decorate each glass with two raspberries.

SCOTCH PANCAKES

My grannie used to make these on Shrove Tuesday, the day before Ash Wednesday, which is the start of Lent. Traditionally, this was the day when perishable ingredients had to be used up before Lent began as it was a period of fasting that lasted until Easter. They are not crêpes or what are commonly called pancakes in most countries but more like a North American pancake. Grannie's pancakes would be white as she did not include an egg but added a little extra milk. They are best served with butter or honey or jam. If you wish to serve them with a savoury topping, do not add the sugar but add a pinch of salt instead.

INGREDIENTS:
MAKES ABOUT 15 PANCAKES
125g (5oz) plain white flour
2 teaspoons of bicarbonate of soda
1 egg, beaten
30ml (2 tablespoons) caster sugar
150ml (¼ pint) milk

PREPARATION:
1. Sift the flour and bicarbonate of soda into a bowl.

2. Make a well in the centre; add the beaten egg and enough milk to make a thick, creamy batter.

3. Heat a griddle or a large flat frying pan and grease lightly.

4. Cook the mixture in batches by dropping spoonfuls onto the hot girdle or frying pan.

5. When the pancakes bubble on top and the bubbles begin to burst turn and cook on the other side.

6. Cook for another 2 to 3 minutes, until golden brown.

7. While cooking the rest of the mixture store the cooked pancakes in a clean, warm tea towel. Best served warm.

MURDERS

TERRIBLE HAPPENINGS ON THE STREETS OF GLASGOW

McLennan Arch, designed by Robert and James Adam and Sir William Collins' Fountain at Glasgow Green
SHUTTERSTOCK/STEPHEN DENNESS

DR EDWARD PRITCHARD

Dr Edward Pritchard became an apprentice naval surgeon at the age of fifteen and four years later he was working as a doctor in Yorkshire. He had an eye for the ladies and it is rumoured that this might be why he left Yorkshire and set up as a general practitioner in Glasgow in 1860. Mrs Mary Pritchard came from Edinburgh and they had five children. It did not take Pritchard long to became established in Glasgow society as a Freemason and Master of St Mark's Lodge and welcomed into the Glasgow Royal Arch. In 1863 the Prichards' servant, Elizabeth McGirn, died in a fire in his house. The family moved from Berkeley Street to Royal Crescent and then to Sauchiehall Street, where Mary became ill, but when she went to stay with relatives in Edinburgh she soon became well again, yet on returning to Glasgow she quickly became ill once more. Mary's mother came to Glasgow to nurse her and Mary showed signs of recovery. However, tragedy struck and her mother died, and shortly afterwards Mary died. Pritchard signed both their death certificates. Doctor Paterson had a suspicion that Mary had been poisoned so her body and that of her mother were exhumed and post mortems found traces of tincture of aconite and potassium tartrate. Pritchard had also taken out substantial insurance policies on his wife. At his trial he was found guilty and condemned to be hanged. Pritchard was hanged on Glasgow Green and nearly 100,000 people turned up to watch. He was the last man to be hanged on that spot as from 1888, hangings took place in private at Duke Street prison.

DUKE STREET JAIL

SHUTTERSTOCK/STEPHEN DENNESS

*There's a happy land, doon Duke
Street jail
Where aw the prisoners staun, tied
tae a nail.
Ham an' eggs they nivir see, dirty
watter fur thir tea,
There they live in misery, God Save
the Queen!*

(TRADITIONAL CHILDREN'S RHYME)

From 1902 until it closed in 1955, twelve people were hanged at Duke Street prison, included Susan Newell (1893–1923), the last woman to be hanged in Scotland. She was convicted of murdering a thirteen-year-old paperboy, John Johnston, by beating him, strangling him and dislocating his spinal column while he was in her home in Newlands Street, Coatbridge.

Newell insisted on her innocence, blaming her husband for the murder, but he had been seen at his brother's funeral so he had an alibi. Her daughter Janet, aged six, testified against her, saying that Susan pushed the body of the victim through the streets in a pram with her sitting on the top, and the body was dumped in the backcourt at 802 Duke Street. Newell and Janet were spotted by the police as they walked along Duke Street pushing an empty pram and Susan was arrested.

On 10th October 1923 Susan Newell, who was thirty years old, walked to her death in Duke Street prison. Hangings were carried out in private but this did not stop hundreds of onlookers gathering outside the prison waiting for the bell to be tolled, signifying that the prisoner had been hanged by the neck and declared dead.

HE MURDERED THE FAMILY AND THEN FED THE CAT

Peter Manuel (1927–58) was born in New York to Scottish parents and five years later they returned to live in Birkenshaw in Lanarkshire. He started his criminal lifestyle at an early age and by ten he was known to the police. By the age of sixteen he was serving a sentence of nine years in Peterhead prison for a string of attacks. In 1956, when he was not long released from prison, he started to kill and it is suspected that he killed Anne Kneilands by beating her with an iron implement on the golf course at East Kilbride. He was not convicted of this crime as there was insufficient evidence. Later that year, while out on bail for a robbery, Manuel shot dead Marion Watt, Vivienne Watt and Margaret Brown in their home at Burnside in Glasgow. The next year Manuel was suspected of killing Sydney Dunn, a taxi driver whose body was found in rural Northumberland, and it was not until after Manuel's death that evidence to support this case was discovered. Several days later he strangled and buried Isabelle Cooke, who disappeared on her way to a dance at Uddingston Grammar School. Only four days later, on New Year's Day 1958, Manuel shot dead Peter, Doris and Michael Smart in their Uddingston home. Gruesomely, Manuel remained living in the Smart's house for nearly a week, eating their food, feeding their cat and using their car. Creepily, Manuel gave a lift to a police officer who was investigating the death of Isabelle Cooke while he was driving the Smart's car.

Manuel was eventually caught and he confessed to eight murders, but not to the murder of Sydney Dunn. At his trial at Glasgow High Court, he was found guilty of seven murders but not the murder of Anne Kneilands as there was not sufficient evidence. Manuel was hanged at Barlinnie prison on 11 July 1958. There was speculation at the time that he had committed other murders but there was no concrete evidence to support the claims. Manuel was not the last person to be hanged at Barlinnie

SHUTTERSTOCK/CHANTAL DE BRUIJNE

prison; that was Anthony Miller, who was hanged there in 1960.

THE LAST PERSON TO BE HANGED IN GLASGOW

Anthony Miller (1941–60) was hanged at Barlinnie prison on 6th April 1960. This nineteen-year-old was convicted of the murder of John Cremin at Queen's Park Recreation Ground, near Hampden Park. Miller and his accomplice, James Denovan preyed on gay men; Denovan would lure them into the bushes where Miller would attack and rob them. This time Cremin was beaten to death and his watch, bankbook and cash were taken. The legal penalty for murder in the course of a robbery was death by hanging. A petition with 30,000 signatures was presented to the Secretary of State for Scotland, calling for a reprieve from the verdict of hanging, but to no avail. As Denovan was only 16 years old he was too young to face the death penalty so he received a prison sentence.

Destination Castlemilk

GLASGOW'S BIBLE JOHN

In the late 1960s, the Barrowland Ballroom was a popular place for dancing and meeting people. In February 1968, Patricia Docker left the Barrowland with a red-haired man in a suit; not long after, she was found dead in doorway, strangled with her own stockings. Her handbag was missing but, despite investigations, the police failed to catch her killer. The next victim was Jemima McDonald and she suffered the same terrible fate in August 1969. The killer struck again that October. A man in a suit with red hair approached two sisters, Helen Puttock and Jean, and said, 'My name is John.' There was also another man with him who was known as John from Castlemilk. The foursome agreed to get a taxi, but when it came, Castlemilk John decided not to go with them. During the journey the other John quoted from the bible and said how he did not drink at Hogmanay. Jean got out of the taxi in Knightswood, where she lived, and Helen continued her journey with Bible John. Helen was found with a bite mark on her flesh and strangled with her own stockings. Her handbag was also stolen. People were afraid to go dancing and some dance halls almost closed as they had so few customers. Despite thorough investigations by the police, no one has ever been arrested for these murders.

THE ICE CREAM WARS

Sookin' a pokey hat SHUTTERSTOCK/EVERETT COLLECTION

Glasgow's East End once saw daily violence and intimidation between ice cream van operators. This was no squabble over a pokey hat but over lucrative drug distribution territory in the 1980s.

The warring factions fired shotguns at their rivals' windscreens and raided the opposition's vans. When the ice cream van chimes were heard, their customers were often buying stolen goods and drugs as well as a double nougat.

On 16 April 1984 six members of the Doyle family were murdered by arson in the Ruchazie district. Andrew Doyle, who drove an ice cream van for the Marchetti firm, refused to be intimidated into selling drugs from their vans and resisted attempts to take over their territory. In April 1984, the tenement flat where he and his family lived was set on fire during the night and six family members perished, including an eighteen-month-old baby. Tommy Campbell, who had a record of extreme violence as the leader of the Gaucho Razor Gang in Glasgow, and Joe Steel were tried and convicted of these murders and sentenced to life imprisonment with a minimum tariff of twenty years.

A twenty-year court battle by Campbell and Steele followed, which included hunger strikes, demonstrations, political pressure and legal wrangles. In March 2004 Campbell's and Steel's convictions were quashed and no one else seems to have been charged with these murders.

LOCAL AND NAMES CLANS

SCOTTISH SURNAMES

In 1016, **KING MALCOLM III** of Scotland decreed that surnames should be used, as this was the custom in other nations. Clan chiefs adopted names from the lands that they owned, and when the king married for a second time, his new wife, Margaret, a Saxon Princess, brought surnames to Scotland along with her entourage. These included **RAMSEY**, **BISSET**, **BORTHUIK** and **GIFFORD**. Through time, surnames also reflected trades or professions such as **WARRENDER,** (keeper of the rabbit warren) **PARKER** and **GLOVER**.

Clan Kilt pin on MacGregor tartan SHUTTERSTOCK/NIC NEISH

Clan tartan, skean dhu, kilt pin, sporran and bagpipe reeds SHUTTERSTOCK/ANNEKA

After the 1745 rebellion, Gaelic names began to creep into Glasgow and were sometimes substituted for a similar-sounding name; sometimes the **'Mac'** prefix, meaning 'son of', was dropped or changed to 'son', as in MacDonald being changed to Donaldson. Macdonald, with a small d, is a patronymic surname or general surname whereas MacDonald with a capital D means 'the son of Donald'.

Associated with the surnames are their mottos and here are a few examples:

MacAulay (*MacAmhlaidh in Gaelic*) means the son of Olaf and their motto *'Dulce periculum'* means 'danger is sweet'.

Colquhoun (*Mac a' Chombaich in Gaelic*) is taken from the lands of Colquhoun in Dunbartonshire and their motto is *'Si je puis'*, meaning 'if I can'.

Erskin (*Arascain in Gaelic*) comes from the Barony of Erskine in Renfrewshire and their motto *'Je pense plus'* means 'I think more'.

GLASGOW TARTAN

Glasgow tartan dates back to the beginning of the 19th century and appears in the 1819 Key Pattern Book of Messrs Wilson of Bannockburn. It is probable that this is a tartan named after the city rather than a family and devised as a marketing ploy by the Wilsons, who are said to have called

SHUTTERSTOCK/RONFROMYORK

tartans after towns and cities where they were good sellers or where they were manufactured. Nowadays a Glasgow tartan, with mixes of pinky red, green and blue, is woven by Lochcarron of Scotland at their mill in Selkirk, where they produce hundreds of different tartans. You can wear tartan even if you do not have a Scottish name or come from Scotland as there is a good range of tartans that are not associated with a particular clan or place, such as the Flower of Scotland and Pride of Scotland tartans. To find out if you have a tartan, visit **www.tartans.scotland.net.**

Highland Military Tattoo Band, Glasgow, 2010
SHUTTERSTOCK/ STEFAN BOGREN

Queen's Park: The pond in Queen's Park was a marsh at the time of the Battle of Langside and legend has it that the soldiers killed in this battle were buried here and for many years it was called 'the Deil's Kirkyaird'.

Crossmyloof: At the battle of Langside, **Mary, Queen of Scots** made the sign of the cross on her loof, the palm of her hand, when things were going badly and this is said to the origin of the name Crossmyloof.

Central Station: 'Going west from Glasgow along Anderston Walk (now Argyle Street) one would have passed the village of Grahamstown, which possessed only one street, running north and south, known as Alston Street. This is where the first permanent theatre in Glasgow was built in 1764. Grahamstown is now covered by the Central Station, but it is thought by many people that Alston Street still exists beneath the foundations of the station. It is also reputed that quantities of silver were left abandoned in the shops of this street and never claimed!' (from Glaswegiana, by William W. Barr)

The Grand Central Hotel at the Central Station

WALKS

GoMA (Gallery of Modern Art) which was once a Tobacco Merchant's Mansion House

WALK ONE: THE MERCHANT CITY

This walk starts outside the Gallery of Modern Art in Royal Exchange Square, where Wellington sits astride his horse, often with a traffic cone

on his head. The Gallery started off as the mansion house of one of Glasgow's richest Tobacco Lords, William Cunninghame, and although the building has been radically altered over the years, if you walk down the right-hand side, the middle section was part of the mansion house. Go into the Gallery and visit the mansion

Merchant City SHUTTERSTOCK/RUI SARAIVA

The City Hall, Candleriggs

Street; turn left and walk along to the end where it meets Ingram Street and turn right. On your left is the Italian Centre and continuing along you will come to an old church which is now the Ramshorn Theatre and is said to be haunted. Turn right down Candleriggs, the street to which the candlemakers were banished after the Great Fire of Glasgow. Along here is the City Hall and Merchant Square.

The Tron Theatre

house galleries on the first floor to get a glimpse of the interior of this grand house.

From the front of the Gallery cross Queen Street, walk along Ingram Street and turn right into Miller Street. Number 42 is another house built for a Tobacco Lord. On the left of this house is Virginia Court and here was the Tobacco Exchange, where tobacco and sugar were traded. Walk through and you will come to Virginia

Babbity Bowster

Continue along Candelriggs until you come to Trongate and turn left. Here you will see the Tron Theatre and the Tolbooth Steeple. Here the Tobacco Lords would strut about in all their finery, with their red cloaks and gold-topped canes. The gallows once stood near here.

Turn left up High Street, the oldest street in Glasgow, and continue until you come to Blackfriars Street on your left. Along here you will see the Babbity Bowster, named after an old Scottish dance. This pub, restaurant and small hotel was a merchant's house and is attributed to the architects Robert and James Adam. The red sandstone properties nearby are converted warehouses. Go back to the High Street and turn left. Continue along the High Street, cross George Street and on your right is Duke Street, where the prison once stood. The tenement buildings at this junction have sandstone plaques declaring that they were built in 1901

Cartouche on a tenement in the High Street

Barony Church, now Strathclyde University's Barony Hall

St Mungo Museum of Religious Life and Art

by the Glasgow City Improvement Trust. Continue up the High Street and on the left is the Barony Church, now Strathclyde University's Barony Hall. High Street now becomes Castle Street and if you look to your right, you will see the Necropolis on the horizon. On your left is Provand's Lordship, the oldest house in Glasgow, and behind it a small physic garden.

Opposite is the St Mungo Museum of Religious Life and Art and to the left of this building you will see Glasgow Cathedral, the only medieval cathedral in Scotland to remain untouched by the Reformation. Next to the Cathedral are the splendid gates to the Necropolis and as you enter you pass over the Bridge of Sighs into this amazing cemetery.

St Mungo Museum of Religious Life and Art

The Necropolis

This is where this walk ends and you can spend time investigating the Cathedral, the Necropolis, the museum and Provand's Lordship; entrance to all of these is free. There is a cafe in the museum. A quick way back to Buchanan Street is to turn right when you come out of the Museum and cross over and walk along Cathedral Street. Here you will pass lots of buildings associated with the University of Strathclyde and at the end you will see the Buchanan Galleries.

Glasgow Cathedral

WALK TWO: AROON THE TOON

This walk starts at number 30 Buchanan Street, the entrance to the Argyll Arcade, the first covered shopping mall in Scotland, designed by John Baird and built in 1827. It is a glittering arcade, full of jewellery shops. Across the road is House of Fraser, which used to be Wylie Lochhead's and has been trading here since the 1860s. Walk along Buchanan Street and on your left, near Princes Square is Mitchell Lane where you will find The Lighthouse, an intriguing building designed by Charles Rennie Mackintosh, which was once the premises of the Glasgow Herald newspaper. Here you can see an exhibition on the works of Mackintosh, including models of buildings that have never been constructed. Go back to Buchanan

Argyll Arcade

The Lighthouse in the former Glasgow Herald premises

Street and continue along and at number 97 there is a reconstruction of Mackintosh's Willow Tea Rooms. They are very atmospheric but the tea rooms are upstairs and there is no lift. Near Exchange Place turn left into Gordon Street and continue along to the corner with Union Street. The building on this corner is the Ca'D'Oro, designed by John Honeyman and built in 1872 as a furniture warehouse. The Italianate style is reminiscent of a palace on the Grand Canal in Venice. Turn right up Renfield Street and on the left-hand side is Renfield Lane. Walk along this small lane and look up to your right and see the coloured, glazed bricks and terracotta designs. This is the old Daily Record Printing Works, also designed by Charles Rennie Mackintosh. At the end of the lane turn right into Hope Street, and at St Vincent Street turn left and take a look at numbers 142a to 144. This building is called the Hatrack and was designed by J Salmon & Son in 1902 in an Art Nouveau style. It is a tall building, ten storeys high but only 100 feet deep.

The Old Daily Record Building

The Hatrack

Return to Hope Street and turn left and walk until you come to Sauchiehall Street, and then turn left. Walk along Sauchiehall Street until you come to Dalhousie Street on your right. Turn right here and you will find the Glasgow School of Art, a masterpiece by Charles Rennie Mackintosh. There is a shop here and you can book tours of this amazing building. Walk back down Dalhousie Street to Sauchiehall Street and turn left. At number 217 is the Willow Tea Rooms designed by Charles Rennie Mackintosh for Miss Cranston, and this is in the original building, and a good place to end this walk. To return to Buchanan Street turn right when you come out of the Tea Rooms and retrace your steps.

Glasgow School of Art SHUTTERSTOCK/ARTONO

At 1pm on 23rd May, 2014, while students were preparing for their final year degree show, Mackintosh's iconic building, The Glasgow School of Art, was engulfed in flames. Luckily no one was injured but the library suffered tremendous damage. Glasgow's fire-fighters did an amazing job in saving many paintings, pieces of furniture and irreplaceable archives and 90% of the exterior and 70% of the interior of the building were saved. The Government has promised to help with the restoration of this highly significant building, at the time of writing there is no indication of how long this will take.

GHOST STORIES

Dalmarnock Bridge SHUTTERSTOCK/IAIN MCGILLIVRAY.

THE GHOST OF DALMARNOCK ROAD BRIDGE

Dalmarnock Road Bridge spans the River Clyde between Dalmarnock and Rutherglen. Originally the crossing here was just a ford, with the first bridge being built in 1821 only to be replaced by a second timber bridge in 1841. When Glasgow engineers, Crouch and Hogg, built the 1891, five-span iron girder bridge on stone piers, it was the first bridge over the Clyde to have a flat road surface. Over a hundred years later, in 1997, the bridge deck was replaced with weather-resistant steel beams and a reinforced concrete deck. When crossing this bridge on foot or by car, people have spotted a young man with a crew cut, wearing a navy blue, three-quarter-length coat and black trousers. He stands, looking over the side of the bridge, and gazing down at the river flowing below. His manner gives the impression that he might be contemplating suicide. Thinking that he might jump to his death, passers-by have rushed towards him and called out to him to try to attract his attention and, hopefully, stop him from jumping. As he is approached, the young man turns and looks and then jumps off the bridge. All of a sudden he vanishes into thin air and there is no splash as his ghostly body disappears before it hits the river. It is said that this is the ghost of a man who committed suicide here, but no more is known of him.

THE CLOCKWORK ORANGE GHOSTS

Glasgow's underground railway system, the Subway, is locally known as 'the Clockwork Orange' and is

The Subway SHUTTERSTOCK/STOCKCUBE

the third oldest system in the world, after the London and Budapest undergrounds, and opened on 14th December 1896. While digging the tunnels it is said that a plague pit was disturbed in the section around West Street and Shields Road and here an ethereal cloud drifts out of a wall and a small ball of light glows and floats around and gradually expands until it fills the whole area. This is not a peaceful happening as it is accompanied by crashing sounds like pots and pans banging together.

Shields Road Subway Station is said to be haunted by a Grey Lady, who paces up and down the platform, and footsteps, whispering and weeping have been heard here. Perhaps this is the ghost of a lady who fell to her death from this platform in the 1920s. The ghost at Hillhead Subway Station is said to be a lady who is dressed for a good night out, wearing a 1930s evening gown. This singing ghost walks the platform giving it laldy, whistling and laughing.

In the 1930s, when the former Kelvinbridge Station was closed for the night, strange sounds like shouting and talking were heard coming from the platform.

The ghost of a blind beggar haunts the entrance to West Street Subway, and is thought to be that of **ROBERT COBBLE**, who froze to death here in the early 1900s.

DRAMATIC GHOSTS

The Theatre Royal was opened in 1867 and was for a time the venue where the One O' Clock Gang, a popular lunchtime Scottish Television programme, was recorded. It is now the home of Scottish Opera. It is said that this theatre is haunted by a former cleaner who wanted to be an actress but, when things did not work out for her, jumped to her death from the upper circle. Still unhappy she

Ramshorn Theatre

haunts the theatre, slamming doors and moaning. The orchestra pit is said to be haunted by a fireman, killed while protecting the theatre.

The ghost of a lady dressed in green is said to haunt the stalls and circle of the historic Citizens Theatre, which was opened in 1878 as His Majesty's Theatre.

The old church in Ingram Street is now the Ramshorn Theatre. The area that used to be the minister's vestry is now the toilets, and it is said that the ghost of a woman has been seen here and that sounds like footsteps have been heard in the auditorium.

The Pavilion Theatre opened in 1904 and an artist who performed here seems reluctant to leave. TOMMY MORGAN (*1898–1958*) was a well-known entertainer and comedian who played the Pavilion Theatre for nineteen consecutive summer seasons. When he died his ashes were scattered on the roof of the theatre and it is said his ghost still wanders around backstage. A female dancer is said to haunt the dressing rooms on the top floor; perhaps it is that of a dancer who burnt to death when her costume caught fire.

THE BURNING OF THE SERVANTS

The Laird of Nether Pollock, **SIR GEORGE MAXWELL** *(1622–77)* was obsessed by witch trials and bringing witches to 'justice'. He travelled all over the country attending trials, including one in Gourock in 1676. This time, it seems as if the laird was cursed as he was struck down by a mysterious illness with a raging temperature and acute pain down his right-hand side. His condition did not improve and after several weeks

The entrance drive to Pollock House SHUTTERSTOCK/CREATIVE NATURE MEDIA

a dumb servant girl, Janet Douglas, indicated to him that she thought he had been cursed by a woman called Janet Mathie who lived in the village of Pollocktoun. Sir George sent his men to raid her home and they said they found evidence of her witchcraft. Janet, her daughter Annabel and her son John were arrested, along with three other servants who were also accused of witchcraft: Jessie Weir, Margaret Jackson and Marjory Craig. They were tried at Paisley and all but Annabel were sentenced to death by burning; and on 2nd February 1677 at Gallowgreen in Paisley, they perished at the stake. Sir George's illness continued and he died within the year. Janet Douglas recovered her speech and married a minister. The wood near the village (which was demolished in the 1700s) is said to be a witches' wood. Sir George's portrait hangs in Pollock House; a man who was haunted by his obsession of ridding the country of witches.

Glasgow Cathedral from the Necropolis
SHUTTERSTOCK/TARGN PLEIADES

THE APPARITIONS

Two men dressed in 18th-century costume have been spotted in George Street chatting to each other as they walk along. Their conversation seems animated but silent; their lips move but no sound is uttered from them. A shift worker walking home in the wee sma' hoors saw them and they walked along beside him for a while and then, all of a sudden, they disappeared.

A shopper in a Brunswick Street shop was sure she saw a man, dressed in an old-fashioned style, sitting on a chair, reading a newspaper, right in the middle of the shop. Then, without warning, the chair, the newspaper and the man all vanished.

It is said that that one of the ghosts in the Western Infirmary is that of a brain surgeon, **Sir William McEwan**, who refused treatment to an artist who was suffering with blinding headaches. The artist was so upset about this he rushed from Sir William's office and fell down the stairs to his death. The brain surgeon in his white coat has been seen in the corridor that led to the operating theatre.

A ward sister at the Western Infirmary saw what she thought was a patient in a blue dressing gown standing near the doorway of a ward, and then he vanished. She thought he had just gone back to bed until another nurse who had seen this apparition recognised him as a patient who had died a few days earlier.

THE WHITE LADY OF THE SOUTHERN NECROPOLIS

The Southern Necropolis was established in 1770 in the village of Gorbals and here the poor were buried in long trenches covered with boards, which were only filled in when the pits were full. There were mass burial pits for the poorest of the 1832 cholera victims while undertakers Wylie and Lochhead made a good living from

The Necropolis SHUTTERSTOCK/HEARTLAND ARTS

the rich victims who could afford one of their bespoke funeral packages. Some years later, poorer people could buy their own family plot, of seven feet by three feet, for a guinea and pay it up at sixpence a week.

There is a monument in the Southern Necropolis of a veiled woman standing in front of a broken pillar – the symbol of a life taken before its time. Within the grave is Mr John Smith, a carpet maker, his wife Magdalene and their housekeeper Mary McNaughton. Magdalene and Mary died as the result of a tragic accident. On a dull, rainy day in October 1933, they were walking from church towards their home in Langside Avenue, sheltering under an umbrella. When they were crossing Queen's Park Drive they did not see the oncoming tramcar and walked straight into its path. The ladies were taken to the nearby Victoria infirmary but Magdalene died on arrival and Mary a couple of weeks later. The statue of the white lady in the veil is said to turn her head, perhaps looking out for the tramcar that was not seen by Magdalene and Mary.

LOCAL CUSTOMS

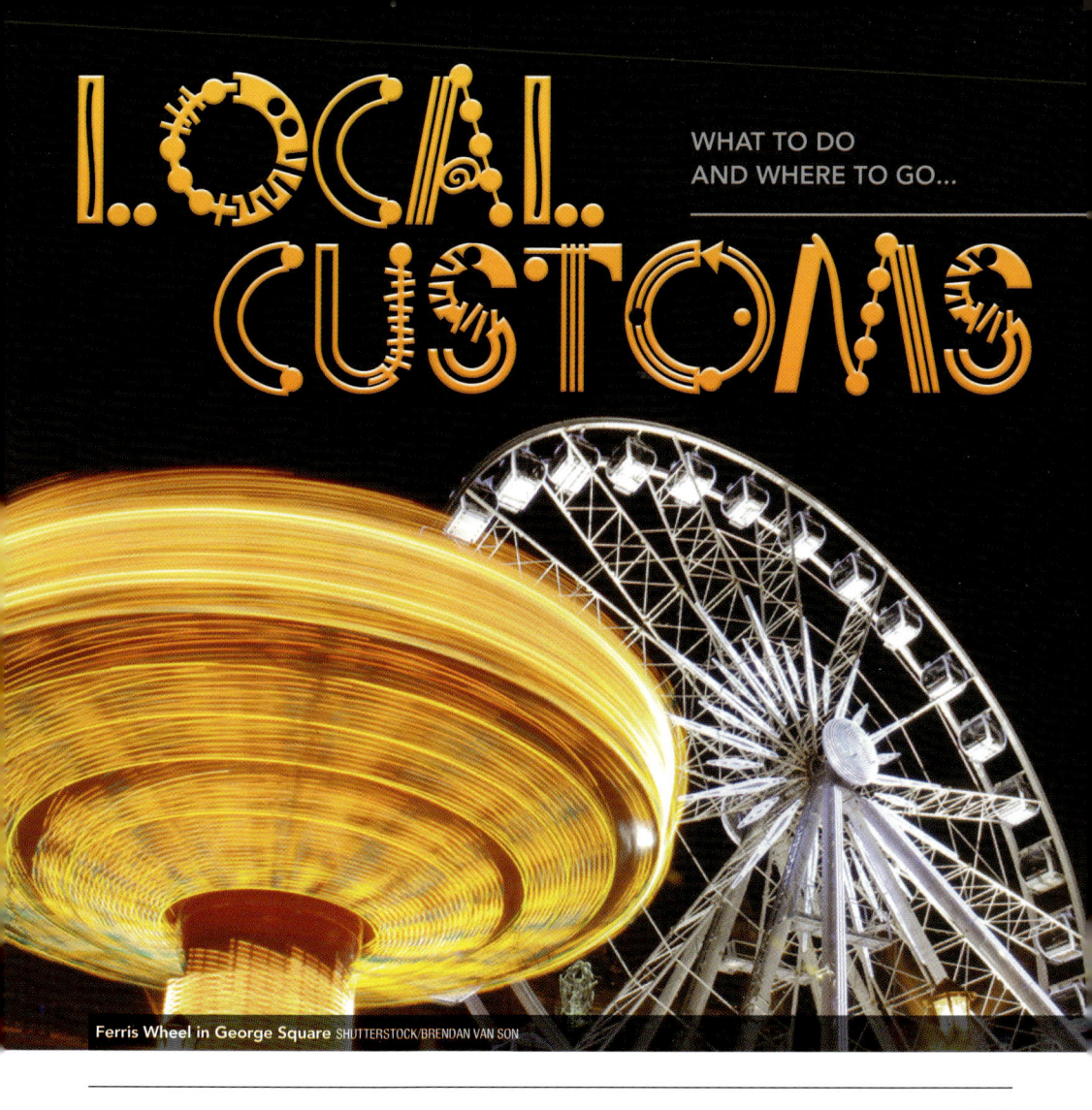

Ferris Wheel in George Square SHUTTERSTOCK/BRENDAN VAN SON

A wee dram SHUTTERSTOCK/ANNEKA

SEEIN' IN THE BELLS AND FIRST FOOTIN'

A guid New Year to ane an' a'
An' mony may ye see,
An' during a' the years tae come,
O happy may ye be.

(TRADITIONAL SCOTTISH SONG)

HOGMANAY is on the 31st December and it is a time for celebrating the coming of the New Year. This can start at lunchtime, as many businesses close early, and a wee dram is just the thing to set the mood. This used to be a family time and we would all meet up at my grannie's house and granddad would give us bairns a Ne'erday present – sweeties when we were young and maybe a ten-bob note when we were older. Grannie would make a steak pie to soak up the wee drams as the evening progressed.

Ferris Wheel in George Square

Ferris Wheel in George Square SHUTTERSTOCK/BRENDAN VAN SON

Everything in the whole house had to be clean and sparkling to welcome the New Year, so the days leading up to this event were very busy indeed. As the evening drew on friends would arrive to see in the bells, and out would come Madeira cake, cherry cake and sultana cake as well as shortbread and a variety of drinks, both soft and alcoholic.

When we were wee, it was a great treat to have some raspberry cordial or ginger wine while the grown-ups enjoyed a sherry or a whisky. As midnight drew near the tallest, darkest and most handsome man would be put outside in the wintry weather to wait on the bells.

As soon as midnight struck, he would be banging on the door to be let in, along with the New Year, a lump of coal, a black bun or Dundee cake and, of course, a wee bottle of the hard stuff. He would be the first foot, the first person to enter the house in the New Year. The first footer would wish everyone a guid New Year, shake their hand and pour them a half from his bottle. This would bring luck to the house and it was said that the family would not go short of food, drink or coal during the coming year. Then some of the family would go off down the road to first foot their friends, and neighbours would call in to first foot our family.

It was an open house, an open close and an open street.

Gardner Street SHUTTERSTOCK/ CLAUDIO DIVIZIA

Traditionally everyone would sing *'A guid New Year to ane an' a"* and *Auld Lang Syne.*

Here are the first and last verses:

AULD LANG SYNE
by Rabbie Burns *(1759–96)*

> *Should auld acquaintance be forgot,*
> *And never brought to mind?*
> *Should auld acquaintance be forgot,*
> *And auld lang syne*

> *Chorus:*
> *For auld land syne, my dear,*
> *For auld lang syne*
> *We'll tak a cup o' kindness yet,*
> *For auld lang syne!*

> *And here's my hand my trusty fiere*
> *And gies a hand o' thine*
> *We'll tak a right guid-willie waught,*
> *For auld lang syne.*

The statue of Robert Burns in George Square, dressed for Burns Night SHUTTERSTOCK/MOUNTAINTREKS

Fireworks and the Clyde Arch

SHUTTERSTOCK/GORDON BENNETT

THE CHRISTENING PIECE

It was a tradition in Glasgow to give a christening piece to the first person you meet when taking a baby to be christened. If the baby is a girl then the christening piece is given to the first male and if a boy to the first female. Babies used to be christened within days of being born, but this is not always the case any more so this custom is dying out. The christening piece was made from two Abernethy biscuits or digestive biscuits spread with butter and sandwiched together with a piece of silver in between.

The silver could be a silver thrupenny piece or even a half-a-crown worth two shillings and sixpence. The biscuits would be wrapped in greaseproof paper or put in a poke (a paper bag). It was supposed to be lucky for the baby and the person who received it. Children would find out when a baby was going to be christened and they would gather outside the close, trying to be the one who was given the christening piece – maybe more for the money than for good fortune. After the christening there would be a get-together and if this was the couple's first baby, the top layer of their wedding cake would take pride of place as this had been saved to be used as the christening cake.

Another tradition was that when a baby was first taken out in its pram to go for the messages, everyone who stopped to see the baby would slip a silver coin under the pillow, a silver thrupenny bit or a silver sixpence or maybe even a shilling, to wish the baby and its mother good health and good fortune.

When visiting a new baby at home it was also the custom to put a silver coin in the baby's hand. The money was never given directly to the mother.

LOCAL SPORTS

CURLING

Curling SHUTTERSTOCK/PAOLO BONA

CURLING

There is evidence of curling being played in the 16th century at Paisley Abbey and Dunblane. The Kilsyth Curling Club dates back to the 1700s and is said to be the oldest in the world. Refrigeration and indoor rinks have kept curling alive whatever the weather, and it is played in Canada, America and Japan as well as Europe. Curling has been an official Olympic sport since 1998, although it has been a demonstration sport since 1924, and since then Kays, who are based in Mauchline in Ayrshire, have supplied the granite curling stones for the Games. Kays harvest around two thousand tons of granite every decade from Ailsa Craig, an island in the middle of the Firth of Clyde.

In curling, two teams of four players take turns to glide the granite curling stones across the ice towards the house, which is the circular target consisting of four rings. There are also two sweepers with brooms, who work on the ice in front of the stone to help alter its path. These brooms used to be made of corn but they are now made of fabric, hog hair or horse hair with a carbon fibre or fibreglass handle. Curling is often called the roaring game which is more to do with the sound of the stones crossing the ice than all the shouting that takes place!

SHINTY (OR CAMANACHD IN GAELIC)

It is said that shinty was introduced to the north-west of Scotland from Ireland, where hurling is still played and Camanachd is recorded as being played hundreds of years ago in Scotland. This sport is a cross between hockey, lacrosse and ice hockey, although it was being played earlier than any of those sports. Shinty was played in Scotland in the winter on special days such as festivals and New Year's Day, when villages would compete against each other, encouraged by the playing of the

University of Glasgow, the East Quadrangle of the Main Building. The University Shinty Club started 1901. SHUTTERSTOCK/ADEK STURGOLEWSKI

bagpipes and a wee dram. It was a free-for-all with as many in a team as could be mustered and no written rules.

It was not until the late 19th century that shinty became more organised and the number of players in a team was set down, as well as some other rules. The modern rules allow twelve players in each team, including a goalkeeper. The curved stick is called a caman and is used to strike a small leather ball with the aim of scoring goals. Glasgow University Shinty Club was formed as far back as 1901.Their team's Gaelic name is An t-Òr is Dubh, the Gold and Blacks. Iomain is one of the Gaelic words used for both shinty and the Irish game of hurling and is now the name of a hybrid game that combines elements of both shinty and hurling.

Celtic Football Club commemoration SHUTTERSTOCK/IVAN CHOLAKOV

FITBA'

It was a Scotsman, **WILLIE MCGREGOR,** who set up the first English football league, and the first international match was played at Partick in 1872 with the Scottish team coming entirely from Queen's Park Football Club. Before the first football clubs were formed, football was played at Glasgow Green and Queen's Park. The teams could have as many as twenty players depending on who turned up, jackets were used as goalposts, players chipped in to buy a new ball when the old one burst and the teams wore different-coloured cowls. In 1867, the Queen's Park Football Club was founded and one of the members, Mr H.N. Smith, wrote reports of their matches and sent them to The Glasgow Herald, which it is said encouraged newspapers to report on football games. The 1872 international was covered by The Glasgow Herald and the Daily Mail.

Ibrox Stadium SHUTTERSTOCK/TREVORB

It was 1873 before Queen's Park Club agreed to supply their players with a uniform and after a dispute about the choice of colours, the kit consisted of a red cap, black-and-white inch-stripe jersey, stockings and white knickerbockers. The new kit was first worn at Hampden Park on 25th October 1873 for the Scottish Cup tie game against Dumbreck. Rangers invited Queen's Park to take part in a football competition on the opening of 1890 season at Ibrox Park but they declined, although an invitation to the club supper was accepted.

Rangers Football Club was founded in 1873 and they played their first match at Flesher's Haugh at Glasgow Green and then on different pitches including Kinning Park and Burnbank before moving to Ibrox Park in 1887.

Celtic Football Club was formed in 1887 and there has been great rivalry between Rangers and Celtic from their very first match in May 1888 at Parkhead, watched by 2,000 spectators, including women who were allowed in for free.

LOCAL HISTORY

LET GLASGOW FLOURISH

Glasgow was founded by St Mungo in the seventh century and the building of the cathedral started in 1238. Glasgow University, the second oldest in Scotland, was founded in 1451.

'Let Glasgow Flourish' has been Glasgow's motto since 1886. It is an abridged version of the 1631 inscription on the bell of the Tron Church which declares, 'Lord, let Glasgow flourish through the preaching of thy word and the praising of thy name.'

*Here is the bird
that never flew*

*Here is the tree
that never grew*

*Here is the bell that
never rang*

*Here is the fish that
never swam*

The Crest of the City of Glasgow on a tenement in Duke Street

The Bird the Tree, the Bell and the Fish depicted on a streetlamp outside the St Mungo Museum

The bird was a dead robin that was restored to life when St Mungo held it in his hands and prayed. The oak tree was originally shown as a hazel branch. St Mungo was left in charge of the holy fire but fell asleep and awoke to find the fire had gone out. He collected some frozen hazel branches and when he prayed they burst into flames. The original bell was said to have been given to St Mungo by the Pope, but what happened to it is uncertain. In 1641 a replacement bell was purchased by the magistrates and this is now in the People's Palace. The fish is a salmon with a ring in its mouth. Queen Languoreth gave her ring to a knight and Hydderch Hael, the King of Cadzow, was unhappy about this, so he removed the ring from the knight's finger when he was asleep and threw it into the River Clyde. The King then asked the Queen to produce the ring but, of course, she couldn't. The knight, who feared for the Queen, asked for St Mungo's help and he sent a monk to fish in the river, where the ring was found in the mouth of the fish.

THE RIVER CLYDE

It is said that Glasgow made the Clyde and the Clyde made Glasgow, both being dependent on each other. The river rises in the Lanarkshire hills and flows the seventy miles to the sea through the city and what was once the heartland of the shipbuilding industry – Govan, Partick, Whiteinch, Scotstoun and Clydebank and on to the Firth of Clyde. The estuary of the Clyde was shallow and the deep-water

Cranes on the Clyde SHUTTERSTOCK/GORDON SAUNDERS

Suspension Bridge of the Clyde SHUTTERSTOCK/STEPHEN FINN

ports were at Dumbarton and Irvine, so during the 18th and 19th centuries the Clyde was deepened and docks were built right up to the city centre, allowing merchant ships from all over the world to sail up to Glasgow. With this expansion of trade the city grew and by the early 1900s it was known as the 'Second City of the Empire', and thirty per cent of all the ships in the world were Clyde-built, a sign of superior workmanship and excellence, an industry benchmark for quality.

Not all the shipbuilders were situated on the Clyde; Alley & MacLellan's Sentinel Works were about half a mile from the water's edge in Jessie Street at Polmadie. They were a of sort of

IKEA-type shipbuilders. The company built over five hundred ships at their works, broke them down, transported them in sections to many locations throughout the world and rebuilt them on site. *The Chauncy Maples*, a steamship, was built here in 1898, dismantled and packed into 3,500 packages and shipped from Glasgow to Chinde in Mozambique, and then hauled 350 miles by barge up the Zambezi River and then by road to Mponda, where she was reassembled and launched in Lake Nyasa, now called Lake Malawi, in 1901. The *Chauncy Maples* had an active life until 1953, when she was taken out of service, but in 1956 she was converted into a refrigerated ship for the Lake Malawi fishing fleet, and by 1968 she was owned by the Malawi Railways and converted into a passenger and cargo ship. She then became a floating bar and is now being converted in to a floating clinic to provide healthcare for the people living around the shores of the lake in Malawi, Mozambique and Tanzania by the *Chauncy Maples* Malawi Trust.

THE QUEENS OF THE CLYDE

John Brown's shipyard at Clydebank built warships and the three 'Queen' liners for Cunard. *The Queen Mary* was launched in September 1934 and served as a troopship during the Second World War. She is now a hotel and tourist attraction in Long Beach,

QE II on her final voyage, Sydney Harbour, Australia
SHUTTERSTOCK/DEBRA JAMES

California. *The Queen Elizabeth* was launched on 27 September 1938 and then converted to a troopship. She took up her role as a luxury passenger liner after the war ended. She retired in 1968 and was bought by a Chinese businessman who planned to convert her into a floating university, but during work on the ship she caught fire, capsized and sank in Hong Kong Harbour. Most of her hull is now buried under the runway at Hong Kong's airport. *The Queen Elizabeth II* (QEII) was the last great passenger liner to be built on the Clyde and a quarter of a million people witnessed

The Queen Mary docked at Long Beach, California where she is a tourist attraction SHUTTERSTOCK/LITTLENY

her launch on 20th September 1967.

She served as a troopship in the Falklands War and retired from service in 2008, and her future still hangs in the balance.

THE GREAT FIRE OF GLASGOW

In 1647, just five years before the great fire, Glasgow was ravaged by the plague and anyone who was able to escape abandoned the city, including the students and staff at the university, who took refuge in Irvine. James Hamilton's house in the High Street was where the fire started on 17th June 1652, fourteen years before the Great Fire of London.

With wooden walls and thatched roofs feeding the blaze, the fire quickly engulfed Saltmarket, Trongate and Gallowgate and by the time the flames died down eighteen hours later, a third of the city had been destroyed. At this time Glasgow had no fire brigade and it was another five years before the city had its first fire station.

Dangerous trades were banned from the city and candlemakers were required to move beyond the boundaries of the city to Candleriggs. More recent great fires have included the one in Ingram Street in 1909 which destroyed the buildings between Shuttle Street and High Street. These warehouse buildings were thought to have contained flammable good such as spirits, wines and clothing.

In March 1960, a fire broke out in a bonded warehouse in Cheapside Street which contained over a million gallons of whisky and thirty thousand gallons of rum. The fire spread to a tobacco warehouse, an ice cream factory and the Harland and Wolff engine works.

It took a week to extinguish the blaze and sadly nineteen Glasgow Fire Service and Salvage Corps men were killed when the whisky warehouse exploded.

Entrance sign to the Barras SHUTTERSTOCK/GORDON SAUNDERS

THE BARRAS AND THE BARROWLAND BALLROOM

Maggie McIver *(1879–1958)* was 'Queen o' the Barras' as she developed an enterprising business hiring out her three hundred barrows from her yard at Marshall Lane. She came up with the idea of building an enclosed market in Moncur Street and the Barras is now a mix of street markets, indoor markets, shops and pubs. Every Christmas Maggie gave all the hawkers a free meal, a dance and a drink. In 1934, she was unable to book her usual hall so she built her own Barrowland Ballroom and it opened just in time on Christmas Eve. By 1948, the dance floor in the Barrowland Ballroom held 2,000 dancers. It was a very popular venue and the queues would line the Gallowgate, Gibson Street and Moncur Street on a Friday night. Barrowland is now a legendary rock concert venue with amazing acoustics and a sprung dance floor that is said to have tennis balls cut in half underneath it.

THE TOBACCO LORDS

These wealthy merchants profited from trade with the tobacco plantations in Virginia, Jamaica, Tobago and Antigua between 1707 and the American War of Independence of 1775 to 1783. Glasgow was an excellent place to ply this trade as the sailing time to America was twenty days shorter from here than from London. Streets in the city reflect the influence of these countries and also the names of the Tobacco Lords such as Dunlop Street (James Dunlop), Ingram Street (Archibald Ingram) and Glassford Street (John Glassford). It is harder to find buildings associated with this trade but there is still the tobacco merchant's house at 42 Miller Street where Robert Findlay lived from 1780 to 1802. The foyer of Glasgow's Gallery of Modern Art used to be part of Tobacco Lord William Cunninghame's mansion house and the Buchanan Street entrance to the Argyle Arcade was once part of a tobacco merchant's house.

Tobacco Merchant's House

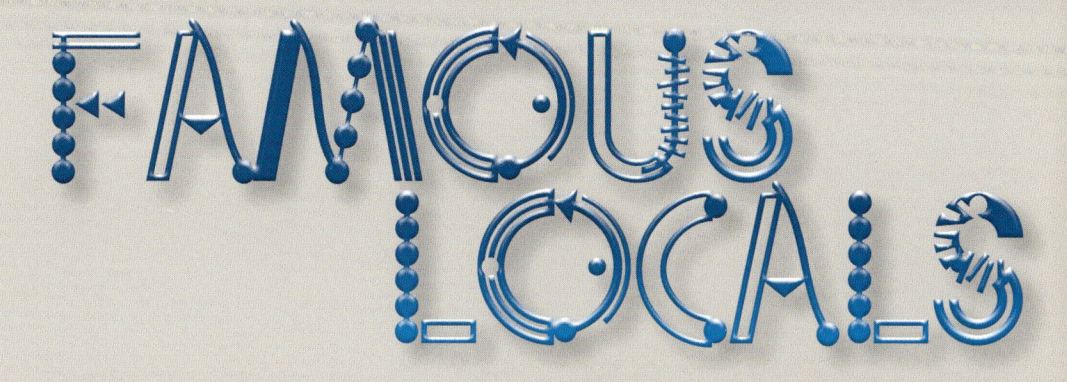

FAMOUS LOCALS

JOHN LOGIE BAIRD *(1888–1946)* was born in Helensburgh and studied at Glasgow University. After serving as an engineer during the First World War, he emigrated to the West Indies and sold jam. He then moved to Hastings in Sussex and worked on transmitting pictures, using scrap materials such as a tea chest, a biscuit tin, sealing wax and bicycle accessories. In 1927, a signal was transmitted from London to Glasgow and the following year he set up the Baird Television Development Company Ltd and transmitted signals from London to New York. By 1932, the BBC had taken over programme transmissions. Marconi in the USA were developing electronics and these would supersede Baird's work by 1937. Baird continued with his inventions, developing fibre optics and radio direction-finding equipment.

Glasgow University, whose cloisters were constructed by George Gilbert Scott in the 1870s SHUTTERSTOCK/MARIA GAELLMAN

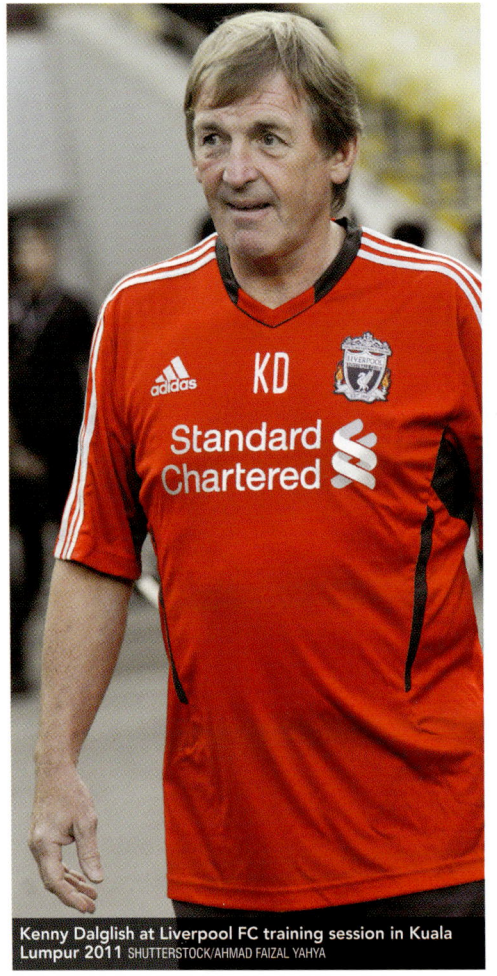
Kenny Dalglish at Liverpool FC training session in Kuala Lumpur 2011 SHUTTERSTOCK/AHMAD FAIZAL YAHYA

KENNETH MATHIESON DALGLISH MBE was born in Dalmarnock in Glasgow in 1951, and brought up in Milton and then in Govan. While still at school he was selected for the Scottish Schoolboys' football team. In 1967 Dalglish signed up with Glasgow Celtic and by 1971 he was playing in the first team.

In 1977 he moved to Liverpool but the Celtic fans were unhappy about this and booed him when he returned to play a testimonial match. However, in 1999 he was appointed Director of Football at Celtic and became manager the following year. During his career he has also been manager of Liverpool (twice), Blackburn Rovers and Newcastle United.

In 1983 he was voted European Footballer of the Year and is Scotland's most capped player with 102 appearances; he has won 32 cups.

Katherine Grainger at the Women of the Year Awards in London 2012 SHUTTERSTOCK/LANDMARKMEDIA

KATHERINE GRAINGER CBE

was born in Glasgow in 1975 and attended Bearsden Academy. She has an Honours Law degree from Edinburgh University, a PhD in Medical Law from Glasgow University and is a Fellow of Kings College, London. She took up rowing in 1993 and is now Britain's most successful female rower. She won her fist silver Olympic medal in the Women's Quad event at the Sydney Games in 2000 and since then she has won silver at both the 2004 Athens and 2008 Beijing Olympics. In the London 2012 Olympics, Grainger won her gold medal alongside Anna Watkins in the Women's Double Sculls event. Between 2003 and 2011 she won six gold medals and a silver in the Rowing World Championships.

The Mackintosh SHUTTERSTOCK/BLURAZ

CHARLES MACINTOSH (1766–1843),

a Glaswegian chemist, experimented with by-products of tar and naphtha and worked out how to bond rubber with cloth. The process of making his waterproof cloth was patented in 1823. He set up his own waterproofing company in Glasgow in 1834 and later went into partnership with Thomas Hancock, a clothes manufacturer in Manchester, making waterproof coats for everyday wear. The drawback was that these coats had a strange smell and melted in the heat, but eventually by working with George Hancock these problems were solved. These raincoats are still called 'mackintoshes' or 'macs' for short. Macintosh also invented a bleaching powder along with Charles Tennant and worked on a hot-blast process to produce high-quality cast iron with James Neilson.

ANDY BARRON MURRAY OBE, the tennis player, was born in Glasgow in 1987. He comes from a sporting family as his brother, Jamie is also a professional tennis player and his grandfather, Roy Erskine, was a professional footballer. Murray attended school in Dunblane and then studied at the Schiller International School in Barcelona, and trained with

Andy Murray practises during the 2012 Australian Open SHUTTERSTOCK/NEALE COUSLAND

Emilio Sanchez, the world number one doubles player.

In 2004, he won the US Open Tennis Boys' title and the BBC Young Sports Personality of the Year. Murray won a gold medal in the men's singles at the 2012 Olympic Games and a silver medal in the mixed doubles. In the same year he also won the US Open and he became the first British man to win the Wimbledon men's singles for 77 years in 2013.

WILLIAM THOMSON, LORD KELVIN (1824–1907) was born in Belfast; his grandmother was Elizabeth Patison of Kelvin Grove in Glasgow. His father was appointed chair of mathematics at Glasgow in 1832 and William attended lectures from a young age. He went on to study at Cambridge and Paris.

In 1846, Thomson was appointed professor of natural philosophy at Glasgow, a post he held for over fifty years. He created the first physics laboratory in Britain at Glasgow University and along with Faraday he introduced the concept of the electromagnetic field.

He developed the idea of an absolute zero temperature and the Kelvin scale is named after him. He developed a maritime compass, and invented a tide machine and depth-measuring equipment. His house in Glasgow was the first to be lit by electric light.

SIR ALEX FERGUSON was born in Glasgow in December 1941 and brought up in Govan.

Sir Alex Ferguson at a press conference before the Champions League game between CFR Cluj and Manchester United on 2012 SHUTTERSTOCK/MELIS

He attended Broomloan Road Primary School and Govan High School and went on to work in the shipyards. His football career started as an amateur with Queen's Park in 1957 and he played as a professional footballer with St Johnstone, Dunfermline, Rangers, Falkirk and Ayr United. From here he went on to become one of the most successful football managers in Britain, winning 49 trophies with St Mirren, Aberdeen and Manchester United.

He retired as a football manager at Manchester United in 2013 but remained at the club as a director. A statue of Sir Alex, designed by Scottish sculptor, Philip Jackson, was unveiled at Old Trafford in November 2012.

WET WET WET is a pop rock group that was formed in 1982 at Clydebank High School, although at that time they were called Vortex Motion. Graeme Clark, Tommy Cunningham, Neil Mitchell and Mark McLachlan made up the group and later they were joined by Graeme Duffin. Their first live performance in 1985 was in the Barrowland Ballroom and the owner of Barrowland, Elliot Davis, became their manager. The band changed their name to Wet Wet Wet and McLachlan changed his name to Marti Pellow.

Their first number one hit was a cover version of the Beatles *With a Little Help from my Friends* but the single that really made it for them was *Love is All Around* in 1994 as it topped the British charts for fifteen weeks.

The Hydro, Glasgow. Wet Wet Wet have played there
SHUTTERSTOCK/TARGN PLEIADES